Through My Eyes...
Through My Soul...Into Me...

by Josephine Landey

Through My Eyes
"Through my soul..Into Me..."

Copyright ©2013 by Josephine Landey
Illustrations ©2013 by Josephine Landey
Cover Photo by Josephine Landey

Through My Eyes is a collection
of original poetry and artwork.

Published by:
Alaska Dreams Publishing
www.alaskadp.com

First Printing November, 2013

ISBN numbers:
ISBN-13: 978-0-9855588-9-5
ISBN-10: 098555889X

For E-Book versions visit the website at:
www.alaskadp.com for links.

Table of Contents

"Sometimes we must travel many paths of darkness...

...before we can see the light...

Dedication

This book Is dedicated in loving memory of
Dolores Landey, Rudy Landey, Eric William
Moe, and all those who touched my life
and are no longer with us in this world.

Acknowledgements

Special Thanks To Steve and Bev Landey, Robert and Joyce Jacobson, Ron Jacobson, Steve Jacobson, Robert Jacobson Jr., Christina Axford, Sierra Campbell, Jeremy Holt, Bill Selander, Leah Laplant, Mathew Phelps, and others whom have been special to me in my life, and all the amazing people who have helped in supporting me through the years.

"I have faced challenges in life of mental health issues and other disabilities. I have used writing as a release and a way to express myself despite these challenges. I would like to say to anyone who is also struggling in life to follow your dreams and your heart and to realize anything is possible. To all those who have supported my dreams and believed in me, I offer a heartfelt thank you."

From the Author

I'd like to clarify that I did not intend for this book to be traditional in any way. I feel like it's an expression and extension of myself and have chosen to write outside the box.

This book is intended to convey an emotional point of view, a mindscape I have felt and interpreted into my own words.

Perhaps this book will inspire even just one person, as I was inspired by the world around me and find the beauty in stranger things.

It is not intended to be taken too literally. It is just my point of view.

Thank you and enjoy.

Forever Strange Without Shame
Josephine "Chaos Kataleana" Landey

A

Josie Landey

Abortion

I'll take this knife and stab your
soul as I take the life that is within me.
I slash my eyes to blind myself
for what I've done.
Look at me and you can see the
monster I have become.

An Angel Lost (Alt.)

She's dying in my arms. The blood flows
upon the cold, cold ground.
My eyes fill with tears of pain and only
these memories remain as my
love dies and fades away.

I feel so shattered.
Nowhere now can I go.
No comfort will I find tonight.

I must it seems be forsaken
from the light
for these things I was blamed
for but did not do.

Why can they not hear the truth
that screams out to them?
Why do they close their eyes and
believe these lies?
Still they choose
to condemn me to the dark.
It seems so lonesome now in
this place without
my precious angels face. Now I am
alone and lost here forever without
my angels grace.

Josie Landey

An Angel Lost (Original)

She's dying in my arms.
The blood flows
upon the cold ground.
My eyes fill with tears of pain and
only these memories remain as
my love dies and fades away.

I feel so shattered.
Nowhere now can I go.
No comfort will I find tonight.

I must it seems be forsaken from the light for
these things I was accused of but did not do.
Why can't they hear the truth that is screaming
out to them?
Why do they close their eyes and believe the lies?
They condemn me to the
darkness. It seems so lonesome now in this place
without my angels smile and pretty face.
I am now lost forever here without her grace.

Another (Alt.)

Still it is just another time, and just
another place. Here it is another sorrow
yet just another face.
Nothing more for me here than crimson
blood and torn lace.
I find myself lost in another
sad and lonely face.

Another (Original)

Another time, another place. Another
sorrow, another face. Nothing more than
crimson blood and torn lace. I am lost in
another sad and lonely face.

As Humans play

Crawling and creeping as I am weeping.
Falling from heaven they ripped out my wings.
Into the darkness now do I plummet with
no one to catch me as I'm falling.
Deeper and deeper the feeling like a
creeper it enters into my soul.
Why must they stab me ever so deeper?
Why do they laugh at my pain?
Such is the nature that is called human.
Such is nature of human so dark.
Killing and forcing and brutally raping us all
but still we stand and play our parts.
We are puppets that are only fools.
Twisting and dancing around on the stage
as we are held up by strings of pain.

A Ravens Kiss (Alt.)

The day has past unto the night as the beauty
of stars hang in soft twilight.
The moon as pure as the fresh white snow
lies cradled gently in the night sky.
I can feel the soft feathers brush upon me.
I listen and I hear the sweet gentle call from
the raven's mouth.
I hear the raven calling evermore
to me and as it calls to me I am set free.
Yes the cry sets me free forever more through
eternity.

Josie Landey

A Ravens Kiss (Original)

The day has past into the night and the beauty
of stars hang in sweet twilight. The moon lies
gently in the night sky.
I feel the soft brush of feathers upon me.
I hear the gentle cry from the soft sweet mouth of
the raven
as it calls to me I am set free. Let me be free
forever more through eternity.

B

Bad Mind (Alt.)

There just itty bitty thoughts in
an itty bitty mind.
Such an itty bitty body all curled up inside.
There is nowhere to run and nowhere to hide.
I feel something dying inside.
Feel that cold and empty
feeling arrive. Left alone so down and out.
Why can't I be at peace?
Where is my promised release?
You see the pain but can't see through the dark
truth in it all.
You cannot comprehend me now. Still more
itty bitty thoughts in an itty bitty mind with this
body all curled up inside. Why do I try?
Why must I cry?
Why do I feel like I die inside when
you try and lie to me? Can you not see the things
your stupidity does to me?
You kill me with this pain.

Bad Mind (Original)

Itty bitty thoughts, itty bitty mind, itty bitty
body all curled up inside. Nowhere to run,
nowhere to hide.
I feel like something is dying inside.
I feel so cold and empty now. I'm always so
down and out.
When will I be at peace?
Where is my sweet release?
You see my pain but still you're blinded
by the dark truth of it all. You can't comprehend
me now.
Itty bitty thoughts, itty bitty mind, itty bitty body
all curled up inside. Why do I try? Why do I cry?
Why do I feel like I die inside
when you try to lie to me?
Can't you see your stupidity is killing me?
When will it end? Back the fuck off before I go
crazy again.

Ballroom (Alt.)

Dance alone to the ghostly music echoing in
the bare ballroom. Hear it as it echoes through
the halls and down the corridors. So alone
now I dance. I wish and wait so long to be
held by another. I'm waiting and wishing still
hoping in dreams that one will come to share
this dance with me.
But until that day this ghostly
soul is damned to dance alone.

Ballroom (Original)

Dance to the music in the empty ballroom
as it echoes through the halls.
I am alone dancing, wishing to
be held by another.
I'm wishing I had a partner to share this dance
but alas
I am doomed to dance alone.

Battlefield Memories (Alt.)

Watch, the blood as it rains down, down, down
from the heavens. See the bodies now as
they hit the cold battlefield. The heavens now
have turned so dark and gray as the soldiers
die this day. Now they are forgotten left
alone beneath cold, cold, dirt and stone.

Josie Landey

Battlefield Memories (Original)

Watch the blood rain down from the sky.
The bodies hit the battlefield. The sky is so dark
and gray as the people die today. Now I'm alone
beneath cold, cold stone.

Beaten (Alt.)

Black and blue, yes it's true I am
going to beat on you.
I am Bloody and bruised because of you…
You make me wonder what it was I did to you.
I will never confess it wasn't you that is wrong.
I cannot admit to being sick.
It drives me on to hurt you more.
I tell them "I can't help it".
I beg of you to stop as you lay again
your hands on me.
I wish you would stop so you could
see what it is you do to me…

Josie Landey

Beaten (Original)

Black and blue, yes it's true I am gonna beat
the hell out of you.
I'm Bloody and bruised because of you.
It makes me wonder "what did I do?"
I must confess you didn't do anything wrong.
I guess I have a sickness
that keeps driving me on.
I can't help what I do. It's really not you
this I swear is true.
Please I beg of you stop hurting and beating me.
If you don't then you won't see all the things
you've done to me.

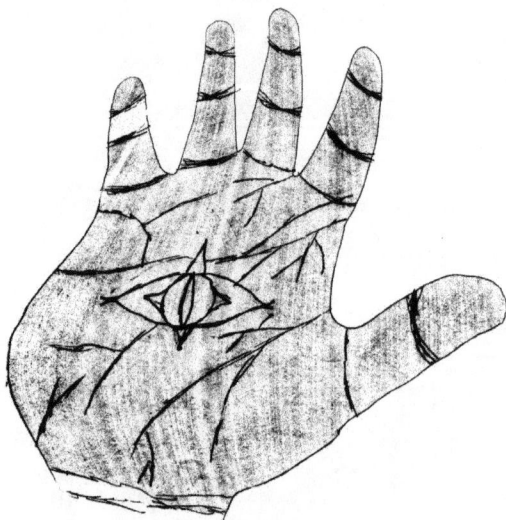

Betrayal of the Soul (Original)

What is the reason for this
stabbing pain inside me?
I try to live within the light but still
I feel so trapped beneath the darkness.
Suddenly I realize what this terrible pain within
me is…

Betrayal of the Soul (Hidden alt. version)

The reason for this stabbing pain is
because I try and live.
I feel so trapped beneath
this darkness, my darkness.
This terrible pain within me is
the pain of death and despair.

Josie Landey

Bloods Rain

Down, down, down it falls all around me. Blood
falls upon me now like a warm sticky red rain.
I feel the red, red rain and the dark
pain it brings as it falls
all around and upon me.
I know the reason and its
reason is me.
I kill the world around me just to watch
it bleed. I kill because I feel the need to watch
them bleed…

Black Mask (Alt.)

So I die and also cry a little inside.
Yes I know that
I turn to the world and offer a smile and
laughing face.
I stand alone in a cold, cold place with a mask
upon my face. I try to choke the words out that
I am okay. I know the truth of the world today.
I feel myself dying a little inside more and more
with each passing day. I can feel my mind slowly
start to decay. Maybe someday
I will be better but just not today.

Black Mask (Original)

Dying inside, crying inside. I turn to the
world a smile and offer a laughing
face standing in
this cold, cold place with this
mask upon my face.
I try to say that I'm okay.
I know the truth of the world today.
I feel myself dying a little inside more each day.
I slowly feel my mind decay.
Maybe somewhere someday
I'll be okay.

Josie Landey

Blood Ashes

Ashes to ashes and dust to dust it will be.
The brave to the grave to mold and must.
So ashes to ashes and still just dust to dust.
Red, black and blue
there is nothing you could do.
Red black and blue nothing more for you.,

Blood Insanity (Alt.)

This blood and pain is all still the same. As I cry
they tell me not to and to have no fear.
They lie to me as
they say everything will be fine. Oh but I
know they can't see the madness that
grows within me. Yes my screams once
again fall upon deaf ears. So here I am left alone
to wither and die within myself forever
through the years.

Blood Insanity (Original)

The blood and pain is all the same. I cry
now and they tell me not to whine or fear,
that everything is fine. But I know they can't see
this insanity building up inside me. My screams
fall upon deaf ears again and again. I am
left alone to wither and die alone inside myself
through the years.

Josie Landey

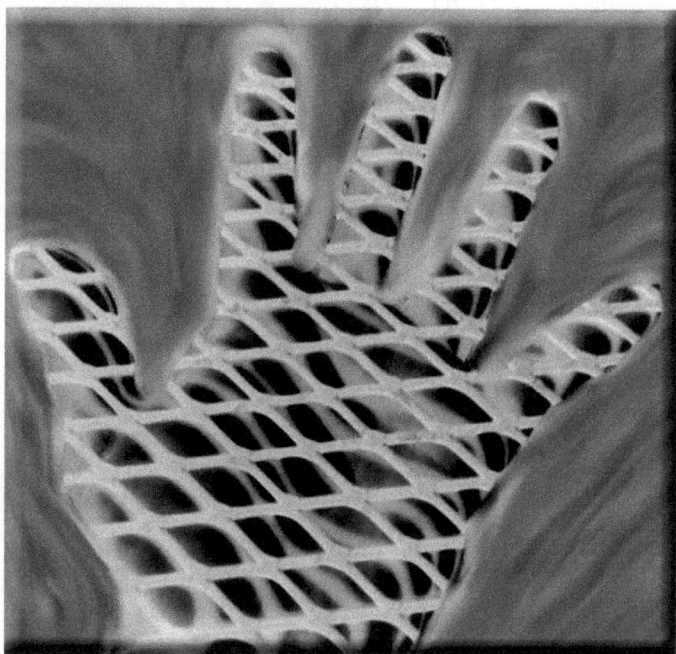

Broken Home (Alt.)

Sorrow, shame and pointless blame are all that
lingers here.
They give us nothing but broken hearts and
shattered dreams.
This home is empty even though
they live here. When they fight I am left alone
and scared because their love they will not share.

Broken Home (Original)

Sorrow and shame and empty blame.
They leave nothing but broken hearts, shattered
dreams and empty homes. When they fight I am
alone and scared because their love they refuse
to share.

Josie Landey

Josie Landey

Contradiction (Alt.)

You are wrong but still you think your right.
You say it is day
but you cannot see it's really the night.
You say that this is life that you have but it is
a lie and in truth is death. You claim to be the
yin but are really the yang.
You think things are different but there still the
same.

Contradiction (Original)

You're wrong but your right.
It's day but its night.
It's life but its death. It's yin but its yang.
It's different but it's the same.

Contradictions He Said (Alt.)

I know he is wrong
although he thinks he is right.
He swears it's the day when it's really the night.
He said all I need is some time to change my
contradicting ways.
But still he is right when he is wrong.
So still it is the day though the night has come.
Yes life is what he called it though it is nothing
more than death. So it is again yin only in truth
is yang. Yet so very different although nothing
has changed.
So she gave him time and time again
over and over.
But wait look at what he has done.
Now It is too late for change cause she is dead
just dead.

Josie Landey

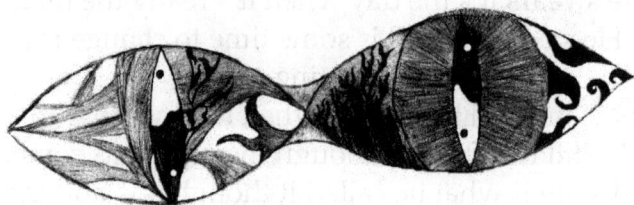

Contradictions He Said (Original)

He's wrong but thinks he's right.
He said its day when it's night.
He said all I need is some time to change my
damned contradicting ways.
He's right but he's wrong.
It's day but its night. It's yin but its yang.
It's different but the same.
She gave him time again and again.
Look at what he's done. Now it's too late
for change because she's dead, just dead.

Josie Landey

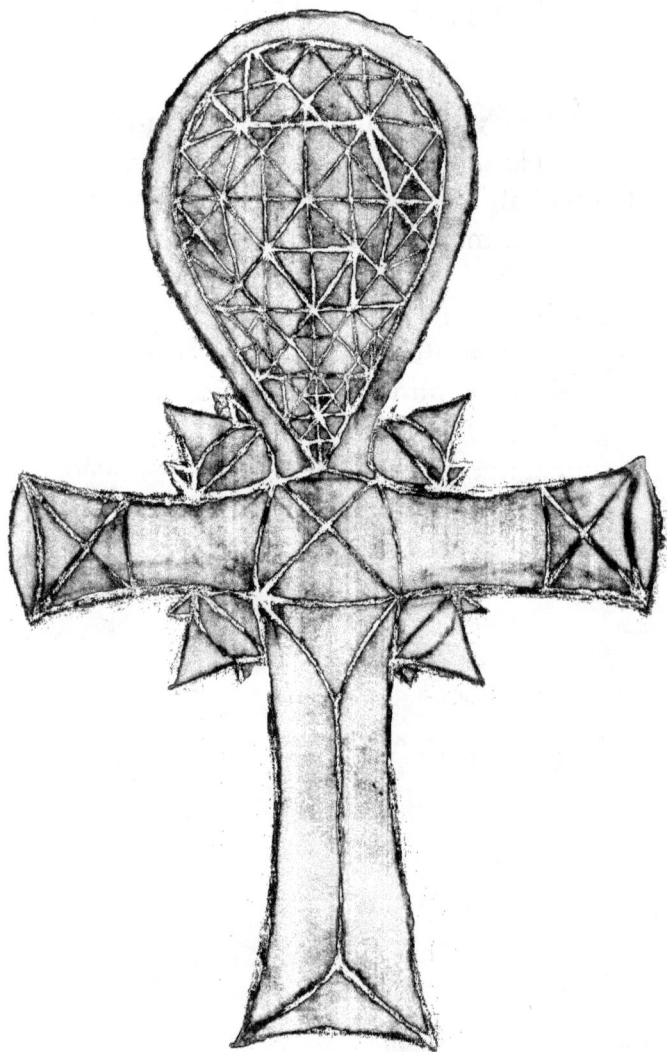

Cry no More for Me (Original)

I've become the thing you refuse to see.
Cry no more for me.
I am the dark beast.
I am the meth.
I am your death.
Cry no more for me.

Cry No More for Me (Alt.)

I've become the thing you refuse to see so cry no more for me.
I am the dark beast but cry no more for me.
I am the poisoned feast, but cry no more for me.
I am the meth that is your death,
still cry no more for me.

Dark Eternal (Alt.)

Once so very long a time ago
I was a happy naïve fool.
Now time has passed for me and
I am no longer free.
I try to run far away but still
the darkness chases me.
Slowly I feel the darkness creeping in
to suffocate me now.
I'm choking in this darkness now and
no one can save me.

Dark Eternal (Original)

Once long ago I was happy and naïve.
That time has since passed from me and
I am no longer free. I try to run away but it still
chases me.
I feel the darkness creeping in and suffocating
me so slowly now. I'm choking in the darkness,
and no one can save me now…

Dead Dreamers (Alt.)

Just forget about the dreamers as you listen to
the schemers selling illusions and telling lies.
Just forget once again all your ties and live in
societies lies. Yes just let yourself go again and
forget about the dreamer.
Eventually you will see
that everything you believed
is now dead within me.
Just one more time you forget the dreamer and
let them die.
Raise the knife and kill it all so you can live
inside the lies.
That's right kill the dreamer and let them die
just to live in the schemers lies.
Just let the dreamers die because
it's all about the lies…

Dead Dreamers (Original)

Forget the dreamers. Listen to the schemers
selling these illusions and telling there lies.
Forget these things and all your ties to society.
Just let yourself go again and forget about
the dreamer, because eventually you will see
that everything is simply dead inside of me.
Just forget about the dreamer and let them die.
Just kill it all so you can live inside the lies.
Just let the
dreamers die, so you can live inside the
schemers lies.
Just let the dreamers die because it's all about the
lies.

Death Nectar

I drink the nectar from the glass now.
As I drain the glass I feel the nectar fill my mouth
so sweet and smooth.
As I drain the nectar from the
glass I feel my life start to pass.
The nectar from the glass has finally
taken hold of me at long last.

Death of a Woman

I saw a woman crying in a corner
so cold and gray.
I saw that woman cry today.
I stopped and sighed today
for that woman who cried.
She seemed so cold and gray, so I stopped
along my way that cold gray day for the woman
who cried today.
Woman why do you cry today?
I cry because I died today.

Death Tried

I try a little... I cry a little...
I die a little each day...
I can't help who I am...
Why must I feel this way?
I try to find the answers... Are these things real?
It is nothing but a distorted
dream lacking any reality...
Please, please set me free...

Demented Lies of Society

Fuck I know it all seems strange how I may
look to the world.
Hell to them I may seem just a little
demented or perhaps even a
bit crazy to all of them.
I know what it is that they think of me yeah
I know, shit they think I am some kind of freak
or demon.
Man they don't know me and
they try to own me and
change me for their idea of
better,
but they can't see that
I'm just me and that their
fucking stupidity is going
to be the death of me, but no
they just don't get it.
Whoever said to
"just be yourself and everyone will
accept you for who you are"
they were wrong because
the world wants you to be good and pure and
virtuous, but
they don't tell you
that they've all completely fucked
up and are all a bunch of hypocrites
that try to judge
people like me just because I look different

Josie Landey

and maybe
because my ideals are different and my religion
is not what they
believe in or they think just because I have red
eyes and black
hair that I am some kind of animal well they can
kiss my ass.

Demons (Alt.)

Demons are dreaming, as they dance and
screaming.
I feel the empty feeling creep deep inside me.
There is nowhere I can run and no place
left to hide. I can't help knowing that I tried and
that I've lied.
I am left and unable to help myself anymore.
Oh such a cold and empty feeling I have now.
I can't seem to hear the reasons anymore.
No more do I understand these things.
I feel I've lost it all.
I wish I could escape the darkness now
before it consumes me forever.

Demons (Original)

Demons dreamin, dancin, screamin.
I feel so cold and empty, with nowhere to run
and hide.
I can't help knowing that I tried. Understand
I've lied and can't help myself anymore.
Such a cold and empty feeling now.
I can't seem to hear it can't seem to understand.
I feel at a losing point. I wish I could escape the
darkness now before it consumes me forever.

Demons Last Stand

I am alone empty and cold. Alone am I in this
world of broken dreams and empty screams.
I can no longer seem to care what it is that drives
me here.
I am but a shell of my former self.
As I stand here by
this pool of water I cannot help myself anymore.
I seem to question what I have become.
Yes I see it now and must
no longer be afraid, but at
the same time I must try and run away from this
pain and darkness that seems to consume me.
It seems in the end all will be made clear for
even in darkness there will still be light.

Josie Landey

Demons View (Alt.)

These foolish humans come
and just as foolishly go.
This is so very true I do know.
I watch and wait deep
within the gates of sorrows, love and hate.
They spill blood and make pain and in the end
there ignorance remains.
Day to day humans live with their lies.
I watch them from far off.
I laugh and cry for them for they could not see
that the time will
come and haunt them through the ages eternally.
Foolishly they
are so blinded by their unwillingness to see the
truth right in front of their eyes.
No more will they laugh at me for what
they do not believe.
What they call a myth is in truth real
they just cannot see.

Demons View (Original)

Humans come and humans go, so true it
is this I know.
I watch and wait within the gate of sorrows, love
and hate.
Blood and pain as ignorance remains.
Humans live within
there lies but it all becomes clear when they die.
They still live their lives day to day. I watch from
so far away.
I laugh and cry for them for they couldn't
see the time that
will haunt them through ages eternal.
Humans are so blinded by
their unwillingness to see what is right in front
of their eyes. Nevermore will they
laugh at me for
what they call a falsehood is truth of reality
they just cannot see.

Josie Landey

Diablo's (Alt.)

See the demons as there dreaming as I can hear
the screaming echo in the air.
I am unsure what is happing here.
I feel so condemned, lost and empty now in
this moment. Still I feel foolish, down and out as
I prowl along down these halls.
I set to running and
I am getting nowhere fast. What is going on?
I keep on trying but I still feel like I am always
dying inside.
I can no longer see clearly
as the darkness covers me.
I stand aside and watch my body fall to the floor
never to be seen anymore.

Diablo's (Original)

Demons are dreaming I'm hearing screaming.
I'm not sure what the hell is going down.
I'm feeling so damned lost and empty now.
I'm feeling foolish, down and out as I wander
down these halls. I start a running and
I'm getting nowhere fast.
What the hell is going on?
I keep on trying but I'm feeling
like I'm dying inside.
I can't see clearly as the darkness covers me and I
watch my body hit the floor
never to be seen again.

Die of Something

We all die of something so pick your poison
well you're still alive.
You know you're going to the dark
side of the moon real soon. You can feel
the darkness creeping in. So pick your poison
well you're still alive because someday soon
you're going to die.
Pick your poison and come dance on
the dark side of the moon, because
I'll be waiting there so I'll see you soon.

Down Spirit (Alt.)

Dance and scream as you dare to dream tonight
beneath twilight. I feel this insanity building up
inside of me. What is it you are looking for?
Still I am lost in the noise and confusion of
slamming doors.
I have left my body lying on the floor left to
wander here no more.
Now my spirit soars so free and
wildly away from me.
Now pain no more will I fear.

Down Spirit (Original)

Dance and scream dare to dream.
I'm feeling this insanity building up inside me.
What is it you're looking for?
I am lost in the confusion of slamming doors.
I left my body lying on the floor
to wander here no more.
Now my spirit soars free and
wildly away from here.
Pain no more do I fear.

Josie Landey

Dying Angel (Alt.)

I see this angel cry inside.
I know why it is she is
dying and she is dying because of me.
Why could I not see what she truly did for me?
Instead I turned away towards blind mockery.
What the hell is wrong with me?
I just do not know why
I did these things. I feel like I am
growing colder and that
my emotions are dying inside me.
I am no longer free.
The demon whispers to me in my
ear and now nothing else will I hear.

Dying Angel (Original)

I see an angel crying inside.
I know she's dying and
it's all because of me. Why couldn't
I see what she truly
did for me? Instead I turned to blind mockery.
What the hell is wrong with me?
I just don't know.
I feel like I grow cold inside and
that my emotions die.
I'm no longer free. I hear the demon
whisper in my ear and
I become paralyzed with fear and
nothing else will I hear.

Josie Landey

Josie Landey

Emotion

I am the emotion distant and sad.
I am the lonely, dark and cruel.
I am the empty, void and useless.
I am the pain, deep and harsh

Eternal Time

Time is the essence that is wasted
on the human soul.
Time is that which passes on
without being appreciated.
Time is the immortal that outlives us all.

Evermore (Alt.)

I cannot help this thing I have been feeling.
It seems like I am so forgotten, so cold and...
empty now.
I am always left so down and out.
I feel so blinded by the pain as nothing
ever stays the same.
I try and it seems no matter what I do
I keep falling to the floor evermore.

Evermore (Original)

I can't help what I've been feeling.
Seems like I'm so forgotten, so cold and
empty now.
I'm always so down and out. I feel so blinded.
I try and it seems no matter what I do I keep
falling evermore.

Josie Landey

Explosive Mind

BOOM! I explode forth from your
mind like a dynamite keg.
I'm the thought that blows you away.
I slip to your lips from your brain.
People stop and stare
as the realize what they hear.
Such a shameful thing said as mothers cover
there children's ears.
I'm the thought that will bring you shame now
spoken blows you away.

F

Josie Landey

Fire and Sword

(An Ode to Valhalla and the fallen)

We crash thru the fire and flames in battles heat,
falling under
blades of steel friend and foe alike. Rise up now
thru the darkness and
ashes of sorrow and shame. Rise up in glory
from the pain.
Let us rejoice for there is naught any more
sorrow or blame.
The darkest hour has passed
now in flowers that mark the graves.
Lament naught for what is
gone has been set free.
So in death we have found glory.
Now we march home unto
Valhalla into the glory
we fought proudly for.
Sing our songs and rejoice
the names of the fallen for
our strength lives on in the
blood and bones of our children now.

Forever the Fools

They crawl out of the
darkness and from the shadows
like slime and filth.
They are nothing but fools to me
blinded by their own stupidity and mockery.
I have seen the past, the present,
the hope and
despair of the future. All these things I know and
cannot say.
There are many days that seem to pass only in
the light of madness for me.
Everyday something new
for me to try and handle and cope with.
I feel like the limits of
my sanity are being pushed
to the barest points of my mind and
are about to break.
They always come so close
to understanding but they
still remain so infantile and unsure afraid of the
truth that I live every day, the pain I can't betray.
Only a dream of peace awaits me in the end.
Until then I hold it all in waiting for the day
I can finally be free of all this mockery.

Josie Landey

Forget

Forget these lies. Forget these lies.
Forget me now. Forget your alibis.
Forget everything forever because nothing is real and
nothing else matters.

Ghost of a Dream Past

I am alone now since I have passed from this
world of gods, kings and mortal men.
I stand by myself watching the world go by like
I was never there.
I realize how futile and insignificant
my life really was.
This thing they call death is only
a release into that which
will bring truth upon the
world and into the eyes of those who once were
mortal and immortal. Now even though
I am alone
I will not be alone long, for none not even
the gods are safe from deaths touch.

Josie Landey

God Help Forgotten

You pray to me when you're in trouble or need.
You cuss my name when things go wrong or
your day had been bad.
You thank me when you win the lottery and
then you forget me again.
Do you even know me?
Am I even real to you?

H

He Said (Alt.)

Some time is all I need is what he said.
Just some time please to change my ways he said.
So time and again I gave she said.
Now see the fact it's too late for change
because she is dead.

He Said (Original)

Some time is all I need he said. Some time
to change my ways he said. Time and time again
I gave she said. Now it's too late for change
because she's dead...

Hocus Pocus Jacks Smile

After dark in deepest night come the spooks and
ghostly frights.
Tricks and treats and smelly feet are what makes
all hallows really neat.
Light the jack 'o lantern and see him smile, step
out now in costume for a little while.
Hear the witches
laugh tonight for this is the time of ghostly
delight. Ring the
doorbells and sing tonight because
Jack has come around to
haunt and bring delight upon this all hallows eve
night.

Josie Landey

Hurt Lover (Alt.)

I had loved a man for many a year.
He made me cry many a tear.
Still I loved him so. I loved him once
but now must go.
True it is I do know that when one
will love it will be the way they go.
This so is true as I do know.

Hurt Lover (Original)

I loved a man for many years.
I cried so many tears.
I loved him so but now I must go.
It is true the love of one you care.
for will be the way you'll go.

J

I Am That

I am the thing you fear. I am the darkness
that you hear. I am the creature that holds
you near. I am the pain in your soul. I am
that which struggles through the years.
As I grow I shed so many tears.
I am your sorrow and pain.
I am your darkness and shame.
I am always here but never the same.

I

I know not fear. I feel no pain. I know not love.
I have no shame. I have no pride. I feel no hate.
I tell no lies. I have not alibis. Nothing here to
remain but these empty memories
lacking anything.

Illusion Lies

I listen to the whisper of the lies in this reality.
I see their dreams become reality.
I know what it is that makes these hopes and
dreams so real.
It's all just a really big distorted lie from the truth
we once knew.

J

Josie Landey

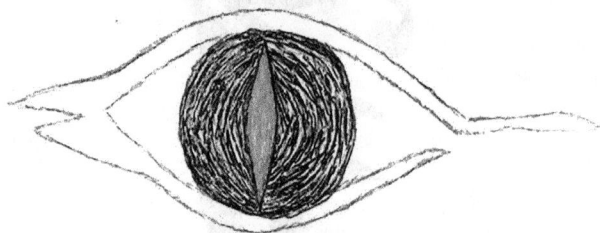

Jerk (Alt.)

Just go away you dirty jerk. Just leave me alone
you jerk.
You're such a jerk to me. Why can't you just
leave me alone?
You're such a nasty jerk.
I hope you go away you bad mean jerk.

Jerk (Original)

Just go away you dirty jerk.
Just leave me alone you jerk.
You're such a jerk to me.
Why can't you just leave me alone?
You're such a nasty jerk.
I hope you die you big mean jerk.

Josie Landey

Josie Landey

KILL

Kill me quietly with the tears.
Kill me softly through
the years. Bury me beneath the ground.
Forget me now like I was never there. Now
I'm no longer here forever through the years.

Kind Death (Alt.)

This brutal kindness is slowly
but surely killing me as
I must hide behind a mask.
So I lie and say everyday
that everything is okay, but inside
it's all killing me and
tearing my soul apart. I guess
I will try and hold on and
bear my pain for the greater good. In the end
even though it will
kill me I will make this sacrifice.
Yes slowly I will die so it will
all be alright in the end.
I die so the world will be no longer
so cold and gray.

Kind Death (Original)

This kindness is slowly killing me as I hide
behind a mask.
I say everyday that everything's okay, but inside
it's all killing me and tearing my soul apart.
I guess I'll try to hold on and bear the pain
for the greater good. In the end if it kills
me slowly, quietly everything is going to be okay
the sky will no longer be so very cold and gray.

Lack Of

I once had a beautiful dream but
it was only a cheap illusion.
I once thought I was rich even though
I had no money.
I once thought love was the only
thing I ever needed.
Now I see all these things are just a very
strange and cruel illusion.

Last

Dance and twirl to the
sweet music of deaths
soft and tempting song. Lay down your weary
head after the long party of life. You are tired
this I know sweet child of light.
My dear sweet child do
not be afraid, I will be the darkness that will tuck
you in.

Left in darkness

I enter this world in darkness.
I live only for the pain because
the madness is all the same. Time and time again
I am left crippled and lame.
I had entered this world in
darkness and I will leave just the same. As I leave
the world fading into darkness
I remain crippled and lame.
As I leave the world in darkness
I have no one I can blame.
As I leave the world in darkness
I am left alone in shame.

Life and Death with Illusion

Once upon a time long ago I believed that life
was the one pure thing. Once upon a time
I believed death was evil and dark.
Once upon a day I believed time was eternal, but
now I see what it truly
shall be that all these things
are just an illusion of being for me all in
the same for eternity.

Josie Landey

Lights of Night

Starlight is shining so brightly
in the darkened sky.
I listen carefully and I can hear the spirits sigh.
Once I thought I was alone, but now I know
that's not true.
There is life, death and energy in all things
seen and unseen.

Light or Dark

Somewhere in the light
this darkness is blinding and choking me.
I know it seems strange for the darkness
to exist within the light.
The darkness is hiding in the light.
Just hiding their
choking and consuming me

Lone Ballroom

Dance to the music in the empty ballroom
echoing through
the halls. There she dances alone waiting to be
held by another.
Still she dances waiting for her partner, but alas
it seems she is damned to dance alone.

Josie Landey

102

M

Josie Landey

Mad Jesters Revenge

Don't laugh at me your majesty.
Soon you'll see what
you've done to me, so don't
laugh at me your majesty.
Soon this jesters going to kill you and then
I'll be the one who's laughing now.

Mad Mind

You say you want to help. You say you really
care, but behind my back
all you do is laugh and sneer.
You don't really care at all for me and
this is all just
illusion anyway… Now I stand here smiling in
your face as
the madness takes its place inside of me.
Well you pretend to
care soon you will see the things you have
done to me and
the insanity that you built inside me.
Now it will truly die within me forever…

Josie Landey

Me

Help me. See me. Know me. Love me.
Hold me. Die inside me.
Cry for me eternally, always by me.

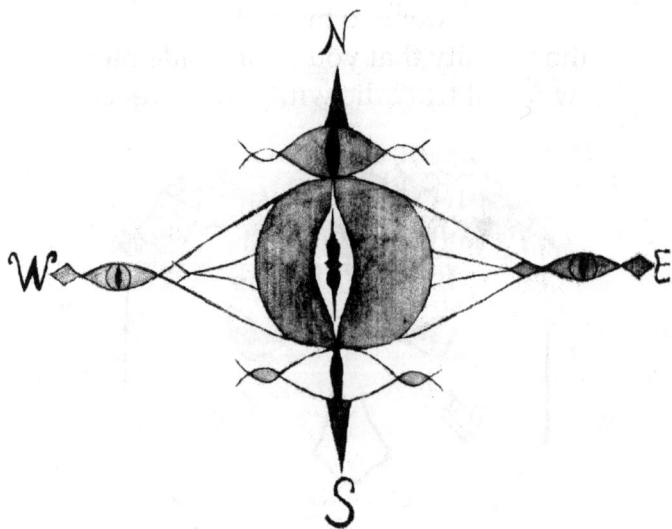

Monster Eyes

How could you not be there?
You turned away when
you had seen what I'd become. You know how
I lied and how I tried. I can't help
what I've become.
Why could you not stay? I never meant for
things to become this way.
You promised me forever that you'd stay but
you lied and went away.
Now that you've left the monster within
will rule the day.

Moon

Softly like a whisper now,
I hear something calling out.
Waiting there soon I'll see
what is waiting there underneath
the moon very, very soon.

My Darkness

To live in darkness is not a sin, for darkness is in
many a thing.
The darkness exists around us in the night, in the
corner and
even under our beds. We ourselves are dark on
the inside
where the light of mortal man cannot pierce.
We must co-exist this way in balance unforeseen.
We are what we are.
The only way we can be more is to
aspire beyond what we know and search in and
beyond the darkness.
This is my darkness and this is my adventure.

My Friend Away

I just lost my friend today. How my world has
turned so cold and gray.
There are no more sunshine rays.
I just lost my friend today.
How I feel so lost and gray. Why did I have to
hear the news today?
Everything was going my way. Alas I just lost
my friend today.
Now I've become so cold and gray.
Please won't someone take me away, away from
this pain?

Josie Landey

Josie Landey

Never Mind

Do not ever mind
for mine has naught a mind to show.
Never mind the sounds of screams
or the ripping sound of seams.
Never mind me at all sitting in the corner bound
in straight jacket and all.
Never mind no not at all
for we aren't really here.
We are just part of the minds of the unclear...

Non-Exist

Sometimes I feel like I don't exist.
These are the times
I wish I could just disappear.
This feeling seems to persist.
I try to interact and be social but they turn away
and laugh at me.
I want to be acknowledged for whom I choose to
be, but for all this
they don't see. I simply don't exist. Well maybe
they would see
if I chose to be that little thing called non-exist.
Would they really miss the one
who did not exist?

One Devastation

A moment of devastation
can shatter an entire nation, leaving
broken dreams and the echo of bloody screams.

Often Dying

Often I feel I have failed.
Often I feel as if I am drowning.
Often I try to run away.
Often I cry these days.
Often I die this way.
Often I have nothing left to say.

Obscene

Obscenities cast at blind eyes remain unseen.
Obscenities screamed at deaf
ears remain unheard.
The hand reaches forth and
slaps the face so numb.
The knife slashes out and cuts the skin that does
not bleed.

Only to Be

To live is to dream so I have learned.
To feel pain is to experience emotion.
To be praised is to know joy.
We exist simple for this is our way.
We only exist from cradle to grave.

Josie Landey

Pains & Illusions

This demon is screaming within me, paranoia
calls out to me.
Everything struggles within me to break free.
I try so hard to keep it all in as I laugh and smile
for the world again.
Inside I cry in pain and emptiness once more.

Path of the Eternal

Forever I walk down this path of darkness.
I walk onward as
the path proceeds winding and twisting
through the darkness.
Where this path goes or where it ends nobody
knows.

Phantom of Madness (Alt.)

Here I stand again still laughing just
the same as I did before.
You could not see that it's
just a game. I will make you
think that you are to blame.
I stand and watch as you try and figure it out.
I stand and watch you as you start to go insane.
You can't shake me because I'm in your brain.
I am always in your way.
I mess with what you say.
I am going to stay and forever I will remain.

Phantom of Madness (Original)

Here I stand again, laughing just the
same as I was before.
You can't see that it's all just a game.
I make you think you're the one to blame.
I watch you try to figure it out.
I watch you go insane and still
I laugh in your brain.
I'm always in the way. I mess with what you say.
This is how I'm gonna stay. Forever I'll remain.

Josie Landey

Josie Landey

Questions Unanswered

What is it I feel today? Why is it I feel this way?
Why are they beating me? What have I done?
Why are they trying to kill me? When will it end?
When did the darkness come? When will it
consume me?
When will it devour everything? Has it really
taken everything from here?
Is it really my fault?
Why does the end seem so near?
Why don't they hear?
Why can't they see? Can't they feel?
Do they even want to feel?

Josie Landey

Josie Landey

Recluse

I hide in a corner and I watch them pass by.
I am the whisper in your ear. I am the dirty little
secret that you fear.
I am the darkness that watches you.
I am that nasty little thing you hope no one
hears…

Josie Landey

Sadistic Revenge

Something inside me just died today.
Now I'm so cold.
I start to feel a sadistic twinge creeping in.
You laughed at me but soon you'll
see I'm coming.
I just want to see you bleed for
all the pain and misery
that you caused me. I watch you
sound asleep and with a grin
I come creeping into your bedroom now.
I've got my knife and rope all ready.
Now I'll tie you up and
cut you good just to watch
you bleed. I promise I won't be gentle
as I listen to your screams.
I promise when I'm done
you'll never forget the pain you
caused inside me.
I'll leave you with nothing but scars and
painful memories for the things you did to me.

Screwed UP!

I did it. It was me. I screwed up.
Yes I screwed up, now
the world can see.
I'm such a fool because I believed.

Shadow

Softly like a whisper he comes in the night.
I know the secret
of why he is here. They ask me why I am so
troubled and yet I cannot say.
He comes every night, looming in the shadows
waiting for me.
He waits so patiently. Still night after night, week
after week, month after
month and year after year.
I know he is waiting to take me to my death and
hold me near in darkness.

Shadow of a Soul

Come now and play a devils game.
Dance to the song of
wealth and fame. Dance awhile when you can.
Soon your soul will be mine to claim…

Snail Sleep

The snail is crawling.
The snail is creeping.
Day once breaking but now
leaving softly creeping into twilight.
Now stops the snail to began its sleeping.

Splatter

Here and there it splatters.
Where it lands does not matter.
On the walls across the ceiling and splayed
across the floor.
I'll stand and watch this madness evermore.

Stalking Madness

They call me stupid, retarded or dumb. But I'll
tell you a secret… a secret
about me. My secret you see is something deep.
For all their insults and
all there ignorant mockery they couldn't see
I'm crazy not stupid.
Now you know my dirty secret and now
they're all going to die…

Straight Jacket Padded Room

Call out softly from within my darkness.
They tell me you are not real.
They've locked me in a padded room
just so they could have a cheap thrill.
They locked me in a padded room just to see
what I would do.
They lock me in this
padded room and now I'm dead just dead
inside… forever.

Suicide Notes

I have felt so many things in my life. I have felt
the pleasure, the pain, the madness, even the
cold depths of the void
among so many other things.
I know none who would
truly know how it is I feel.
Now I cut myself and let the blood
of my life flow upon the floor.
Maybe now they can read it and
understand the misery in my life story as it
slowly spills out onto
the cold, cold ground. Let them read and maybe
then they will
understand that which could not be seen before.

Sunset of Chaos

My mind askew as I watch the view of a demons
sunset turning into the chaos of night.
As I gaze into the wonder of this demonic chaos
I seem to lose myself.
My vision starts to shift and blur.
My mind starts to shift and sway.
I think I'll just let myself drift
away and my mind decay.
I guess I'll be lost anyway.

T

Tears of Bloodshed

Tears of blood pour down like rain down they
fall from my face.
I cry and cry today.
I feel like the pain never goes away.
The sky is dark the sky is gray still my pain has
not gone away this long and lonely day.
My face is so sad and my heart so
broken and torn. Here I am standing
here alone with the
tears of blood pouring down my face.
Please somebody hear my cry and take me from
this sad lonely place.

The Beast

To feed the beast another day
has left me so cold and gray.
Alas alone am I to feed the beast another day
still only to remain so cold and gray.

The Last Prayer of the Damned

Demons dream they dance and scream as the
darkness it comes.
I can't see as it falls upon me that it has begun.
You pretend to see but yet you're
blind to what I've done.
You try and turn away to ignore
what I've become.
I feel the cold emptiness creeping in now.
I know I've lied and seen you cry and in all this
I feel something has died. I cannot ask
forgiveness for what I've done.
Understand it wasn't you it happened to.
You couldn't see the truth coming
now again as once more
I come undone. So let the blood
flow now for death comes
tonight in soft clouded moonlight.

Josie Landey

The Mad Mind

You say you want to help.
You say you really care, but
behind my back all you do is laugh and sneer.
You don't really care at
all for me and this is all just illusion anyway…
Now I stand here smiling in
your face as the madness takes its place inside of
me. Well you pretend
to care soon you will see the things you have
done to me and the insanity
that you built inside me. Now they will all truly
die in darkness forever.

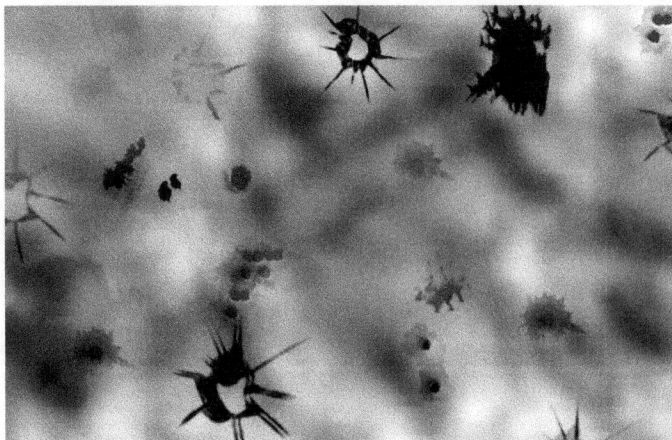

Time Alone

I stand alone here before the waves
of time ever watching
from my point upon the beach.
As the sands are passing
I am here wondering what to do again.
Even as I seek out an answer I am still lost to the
flow of time.
Alas what shall I do? Oh for what shall be mine?

Thoughts of Blood

A thought passed my way today. A thought that
was very dark.
This thought will not go away today. This
thought is so dark.
I see the blood spew and spray.
I guess this nasty thought is here to stay.

Thoughts Eternal

What is a thought but a whisper? What is a
whisper but a dream?
What is a dream but a fantasy and fantasy to
become reality.

U

Josie Landey

Unbidden Demon

Only in a dream could they know me.
Only in a moment
of truth will they feel me.
Only when the light will pierce
the darkest night could they
feel this pain… my pain.
Only when these things are known
will all be made
clear to them. For only until the sun
will refuse to shine
I alone shall dine upon the darkness of mankind.

Under the Sky

Thru the dreams and blood and screams
I feel this wave of
tension coming over me. In my eyes
are blood let tears and
in my ears screams of fear. To the pain
I now turn, and away from things once held
dear I turn again into darkness. I step into the
darkness moving further from the light.
I find my satisfaction
in the life of night. The day hides away
just another lie always trying to reject the black
sky. The day lives only in
death never to reveal its truth and jest.

Josie Landey

Josie Landey

Voided Mind

Listen to the mindless noise.
Listen to the silent screams.
Listen to the senseless ruse.
Listen to the useless muse.

Josie Landey

Walking in Darkness

An ominous melody echoes through
these dim damp halls.
I walk and silence cannot be found within myself
as my mind screams
out for blood, lust, and power. These things
craved should not be.
The beast I cannot sooth as it claws sink deep
within my mind roaring
to be free. Now you see this is the walk of me.

War Mind

Fires burning and bodies turning.
Steel clashing and soldiers lashing out.
Slicing and slashing in battlefield heat.
Nether side wants defeat.
Kings and countries go to war just to
spill blood once more.
I see the lust for power in their eyes.
I stand and see the innocent die,
just because of their war lust minds.

Water

Dance to the dreams as the demons scheme and
angels scream.
I feel the heat beat down upon me like hellfire.
My flesh blisters and burns in this desert hell.
I can feel my throat slowly turning dry
like the hot desert sand.
Please come and rescue me...

Wonder

I wonder where it all begins. I don't know no
more. I can see and yet
I'm blind. I can hear but
still choose to remain deaf.
The world turns onward so it seems.
I see that no one is perfect but
yet they want me to be.
I care no more about their little act or there
pathetic stupid lies. I say no more compromise.

Josie Landey

Words of Hate

They live their lives day to day.
They tell there lies without
regard or compromise.
They pretend to be your friend
as they stab you in the back again.

X-Stream

Fast and hard so it seemed.
Adrenaline flowing and running
freely in my blood.
You can feel it as the rush comes upon you.
You can now feel the point
of being at the X-STREAM.

X-Offed

She walked into the darkness with no
place left to turn.
She set it all on fire and
stood and watched it burn.
She finally had enough when
the pain became too much.
She used to set his world on fire with desire.
The day had finally came
that he had gone insane.
Out the window he thought he could fly but fell
down and only died.
Such is the nature of drugs to suicide.

Josie Landey

Josie Landey

Years

The blood and pain is all that
remains through shattered
dreams and memories.
Through all the years and all these
tears, I feel like I'm alone with my fears.
When you died that
day I cried so sad and alone with my heart
breaking and aching
inside me. Not a day goes by that
I don't miss you, But my
comfort lies within the fact that someday I'll see
you again soon.

Yellow Rose of Death

Turn the yellow roses.
Let the sunshine fall like rain.
There is nothing but this darkness
ending in this pain.

You

You tell me to stop crying
I try to tell you I'm dying.
You laugh at me with your mockery and turn a
blind eye to what you see.
You're living a lie and locking me inside this
dark dungeon of pain.
It's not me. Why can't you see? You're killing me.
I no longer need this cold mockery.
Now I'm gone this you see.
Now I'm free of your blind mockery.

Josie Landey

Zipped

Zip it and just shut the hell up. Every time you
speak the words hurt.
Every word you say makes
my ears want to bleed.
Why can't you just keep it zipped up?
You just never learn to shut the hell up.
Why can't you learn to shut
up and not tread on others?
That's why you hurt them your
words are so damn wrong.
But what do you know?
Nothing is what you know because that's
just the way you are.

Zone Mind

Scream to me your hate and
whisper to me your dark desire.
Take away my freedom and
strike me with a knife.
Slash at me wildly you know you want my life.
In these things is the dark desire and you know it
takes you higher.
Come on and taste that dark desire
brooding from within.
Release the monster from within the cage. Now
you set free your rage again.

Josie Landey

About the Author

Josephine D. Landey was born in the town of Grand Rapids, MN. She pursued reading and writing poetry from a young age as a hobby. She is a high school graduate of Pine River, MN.

This is her first book and she is very excited about the results and expresses a great joy of being able to share this with the world. It has been a pleasure to write and she looks forward to publishing another book in the future.

Thank you for reading this book.
If you'd like to contact me, I welcome your questions and comments.
Email me at: josielandey@alaskadp.com
Facebook:
https://www.facebook.com/sapphire.blackcat

Other titles by
Alaska Dreams Publishing
Inside the Circle
The Silver Horn of Robin Hood
Ghost Cave Mountain

Visit the ADP website at:
www.alaskadp.com

www.ingramcontent.com/pod-product-compliance
Lightning Source LLC
Chambersburg PA
CBHW061723020426
42331CB00006B/1061